TEA AT FORTNUM & MASON

Tea

at

FORTNUM & MASON

PICCADILLY SINCE 1707

EBURY
PRESS

10 9 8 7

Published in 2010 by Ebury Press, an imprint of Ebury Publishing
A Random House Group Company

Text copyright © Ebury Press 2010
Recipe copyright © Emma Marsden 2010
Recipes on pages 77 and 95 © Fortnum & Mason 2010
Photography copyright © Emma Lee 2010
Images on pages 10–34 © Fortnum & Mason 2010

The Random House Group Limited Reg. No. 954009

Addresses for companies within the Random House Group can be found at
www.randomhouse.co.uk

A CIP catalogue record for this book is available from the British Library

The Random House Group Limited supports the Forest Stewardship Council®(FSC®),
the leading international forest - certification organisation. Our books carrying the FSC
label are printed on FSC® - certified paper. FSC is the only forest-certification scheme
supported by the leading environmental organisations, including Greenpeace. Our paper
procurement policy can be found at www.randomhouse.co.uk/environment

To buy books by your favourite authors and register for offers visit www.randomhouse.co.uk

Design: Turnbull Grey
Recipe compilation: Emma Marsden
Photography: Emma Lee
Food styling: Emma Marsden
Prop styling: Cynthia Inions
Additional recipe testing: Michaella Pentucci

Printed and bound in China by C&C Offset Printing Co., Ltd

ISBN 978 0 09 193768 3

Contents

Introduction

The world of tea and the name of Fortnum & Mason have been intertwined for over three centuries. From the opening of the Far East to western trade, to the first harvest of tea grown on English soil, Fortnum's has sourced, refined and offered this most delicious of the Earth's bounties to its customers.

Each generation discovers tea anew, and develops its own preferences. Whether ancient Chinese blends, perfumed teas, or invigorating green or red bush tea, Fortnum's has sourced the best examples of their kinds.

To celebrate this long and fruitful relationship, I am delighted to introduce this tribute to tea and its place in society. Delicious recipes are complemented by the fascinating history of tea, the properties of individual teas and that most traditional of English pastimes – taking tea. If you love tea, I recommend this short compendium for your delight.

Kate Hobhouse
Chairman

The History of Tea

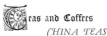

eas and Coffees
CHINA TEAS

Finest Kee Mun China Tea. Specially imported
by Fortnum & Mason. In Oriental caddies
1-lb. net 7/6 ; 5-lbs. net 32/6
Superb Lapsang Souchong -   1-lb. tin 8/6
10-lb. original boxes enclosed in mats
per box 80/-
Mayfort Caravan Tea. Resembling the old
"Russian Caravan Tea"   - *per lb.* 6/6 ;
per 7-lb. *caddy* 44/-
Finest Ichang. Magnificent Tea, to be used
unblended. A flavour that is quite distinct
from any other -   -   -   *per lb. tin* 5/4

PRETTY INCIDENT. *Fortnum & Mason's stud
of Elephants salaaming to the Viceroy*

182 *Piccadilly, W. 1*

Fortnum & Mason's tea selection in 1927

TEA AND COFFEE

All because the Inspecting General had
not had his cup of F & M tea
After Meissonier

CHINA TEAS

KEE MUN	MAYFORT CARAVAN
This delicately flavoured tea is packed in original hand-painted caddies that are well worth keeping for ever after	A very subtle blend of China teas resembling the old Russian caravan tea that used to be imported overland from the East
1-lb. *caddy* 7/2 . 5-lb. *caddy* 31/-	*a lb.* 6/2
LAPSANG SOUCHONG	**EARL GREY**
This superb tea, with the famous "smokey" flavour, is sold direct to you in its original Chinese caddy	We design this to make an afternoon tea of outstanding merit. A blend of rare and also-gether wonderful China teas
1-lb. *caddies, each* 8/6	*a lb.* 4/4 . *a* 7-lb. *caddy* 28/- *post extra*
LAPSANG SOUCHONG	**KING'S BLEND**
Packed in the original Chinese caddy, just as received by us. A caddy of tea to make a present to someone who understands good things	As supplied to His late Majesty King Edward VII
5 *lbs. nett* 31/-	*a 1-lb. tin* 4/4 . *a* 7-lb. *caddy* 28/- *post extra*
DOWAGER	**MASON BLEND**
This is the marvellous China tea we keep on purpose for those who find their greatest delight in the exquisite flavour of Formosa Oolong teal	Ningchow, Kee Mun and Ichang. Delicate of flavour
a lb. 8/2	*a lb.* 3/- . *a* 7-lb. *caddy* 20/6 *post extra*

GIVE F&M HAMPERS THIS CHRISTMAS

forty-four

Christmas Catalogue, 1931

THE ORIGINS OF TEA

Tea originated in China but myth and mystery surround the actual discovery of what was to become Fortnum's finest and most famous offering. One story relates how, in 2737BC, the learned Emperor Shen Nung was gathering plants. He rested under a tall wild tea bush and boiled some water for refreshment. A few leaves lazily drifted down from the branches and fell into the water. The resulting stimulating and refreshing liquor is what we now call tea. A later legend describes how Dharuma, a Buddhist monk, fell asleep while meditating. He punished himself for this transgression by cutting off his eyelids. They fell to the ground and there the first tea bushes grew. Wild bushes may have been the Emperor's choice as a source of tea, but the plant has been cultivated for millennia. Connoisseurs during the T'ang dynasty (618–906AD) crushed steamed bound-together leaves to make a sort of tea powder that was then mixed with a variety of flavourings – including plum juice and onions, the latter being arguably an acquired taste.

Sung Dynasty (960–1279AD) tea drinkers whipped ground tea into hot water until it was frothy, which sounds rather like a very early tea cappuccino. There is no record of onions being added to this concoction, but flowers and essential oils made sure it was extremely exotic. It was not until the Middle Ages that tea drinkers in China (1368–1644AD to be exact) developed tea as we know it today. Steamed leaves were dried, added loose to the water and left to steep, before being poured into white porcelain to display its colour. Drying the leaves allowed the tea to ferment or oxidise to a coppery red, and made it easier to store while preserving its essential characteristics. It also meant that it was fit to travel to far-off lands.

Although tea drinking has become inextricably linked with Englishness, it was in fact introduced to Europe by Portuguese and Dutch traders in the early seventeenth century. Tea had reached London by 1658, although it took the marriage of Charles II to Catherine of Braganza (a Portuguese princess) to make it wildly fashionable at court. The court connection was important in the creation of a certain tea emporium in the heart of St James's …

Dr Johnson and Mrs Thrale
over tea and cakes

FORTNUM & MASON – A RELATIONSHIP WITH TEA

In 1707, livery stables owner Hugh Mason and royal footman William Fortnum set up business together as Fortnum & Mason, grocers and tea merchants. Tea was the commodity on which the two young men built their dreams and grew their business. William Fortnum had family connections that entailed an intimate association with the magical brew; one of his cousins worked for the East India Company, the principal means of import of what was to become the national drink.

Fortnum's façade, 1840

AN ENGLISH BEVERAGE OF CHOICE

It took between twelve and fifteen months for precious shipments of tea to travel to Britain by sea. The costs of bringing the tea from halfway

A special tea flyer, 1930

This is the
WILLOW PATTERN
COMMENTARY

"All the world's a plate
and all the dishes Fortnum and Mason's"

Free adaptation from As You Like It
Act 2, Scene VII

Issued by FORTNUM AND MASON in their
Fine Old Georgian House *at* 182 PICCADILLY W1

Page taken from a Tea Commentary, 1924

across the globe, and heavy taxation, meant that initially only the wealthy enjoyed it in its unadulterated form. By 1707 tea smuggled from Holland was booming on the black market, and much of it was padded out with unmentionable substances. Discerning – and law-abiding – tea drinkers flocked to Fortnum & Mason to buy pure (and purely legal) tea, including strong black teas, that had been created especially to withstand the long journey westwards.

The eighteenth century saw the amount of tea drunk in England grow by a staggering 225 per cent, and Fortnum & Mason can lay claim to some small contribution to the rise in its popularity. In 1784, the government gave in to the inevitable and decided to battle the smugglers by reducing tax on tea from 119 per cent to just 12½ per cent. Now nearly everyone could drink tea legally. It soon became a popular breakfast drink, replacing ale and gin, and gradually it became the drink to enjoy at any time of the day.

The same century saw coffee houses fall out of favour, to be replaced by elegant open-air tea gardens, which enjoyed the patronage of the most fashionable in society. Perhaps the most famous were Ranelagh Gardens in Chelsea, which opened in 1742, its principal feature being a rotunda designed on the Pantheon in Rome. Entry to the gardens cost two shillings and six pence (around 12½p), which – of course – included tea! One of its most famous visitors was Mozart, who played there for the Duke of Cumberland.

THE BOSTON TEA PARTY

Tea drinking took off in America at the end of the seventeenth century and the fashion for tea gardens became popular there, too. In Boston, a major seaport, tea symbolised wealth and social status. America was a British colony at that time, and much of its tea was imported from Britain, including a good share of it from Fortnum & Mason.

In 1767, Parliament increased taxes on tea and other goods in the American colonies to cover administrative costs in the New World. It proved immensely unpopular, and while over the ensuing years taxes on some goods were lifted, the hated tax on tea remained. One fateful day in 1773, seven ships from England arrived carrying tea. Bostonians, many dressed as Native Americans, boarded one of these, the *Dartmouth*, and threw its cargo of Lapsang Souchong (some of which is thought to have been Fortnum's) into the salty harbour. The incident, immortalised in the title the Boston Tea Party, marked the end of Britain's governance of that part of North America but did not end Fortnum's American customers' love of good tea, which continued to be exported to discerning Loyalists and Republicans alike.

THE OPIUM WARS

The early nineteenth century saw the relationship between Britain and China sour, thus jeopardising the ever-growing tea market. Chinese goods were in great demand in Britain, but there was little of British manufacture that the Chinese wanted in

American

Groceries

F&M COOKIES

F&M GOODIES

F&M CORN

F&M CHOWDER

&M SEA FOOD

PRESERVES

Fortnum & Mason Ltd.

181 Piccadilly, London, W.1

REGent 8040

American customers in the 1930s flocked to Fortnum's for tea, while British customers
sought American specialities

Rolling Along – Two Tea Clippers by Montague Dawson

Rolling Along – The Gleaner by Montague Dawson

return. The East India Company embarked on an illegal trade with the Chinese in Bengal opium, and this in turn led to two Opium Wars between Britain and China in the early years of Victoria's reign, and again at the end of the 1850s.

The Wars changed the face of the tea trade for ever; in 1839 almost all the tea consumed in the United Kingdom came from China, but by 1860 85 per cent came from India and Ceylon, and only 12 per cent from China. Once more, tea became expensive, and Fortnum's rejoiced in the fact that its tea customers were amongst the wealthiest in the land.

Personal service, 1957

THE CLIPPER SHIPS AND GREAT TEA RACES

It was the Americans who introduced the streamlined and yacht-like clipper ship to international trade, substantially reducing the time it took to transport goods across the globe. By the early 1850s Britain had its own fleet of fast new ships. They would set off from China for Britain on the same tide and race back to collect a prize for the crew, and a supreme prize for the first tea delivered from the racing vessels.

The romantic age of the clipper races continued for twenty years, until the clippers were replaced by steamships. Tea was no longer a toddler by the time it reached Britain from China and India; when the Suez canal opened in 1869, its journey time meant that it was a mere babe of three months when it fetched up in the basin of the Thames.

Christmas Catalogue, 1931

𝕹otice

⊷ TO THE NOBILITY ⊶
& GENTRY
throughout the King's Dominion
ABOUT

ii TEAS

that *cry out* to be drunk of
DEEPLY
by reason of their
surpassing loveliness

*SUPPLIED By us for many YEARS to HIS late MAJESTY
King EDVVARD VII*

**KING'S
BLEND
*Tea***   IN truth a Royal tea with fragrance that gives sweet amaze to connoisseurs, and a flavour of such beauty as is not to be equalled in all the world. A China blend of Lapsang, Keemun, Ichang and Kintuck.
In One Pound *Tins* 4/8 *each*

**QUEEN
ANNE
*Tea***   THE Queen of Indian and Ceylon teas. We blend it with pride and loving care from all that is best in certain chosen tea gardens of Assam, Ceylon and Darjeeling. It is a tea of gentle loveliness.
In One Pound *Tins* 4/8 *each*

FROM
FORTNUM & MASON
Importers since Tea was a novelty in England
Established at 182 PICCADILLY, *W*
for over 200 years

OUR ARGOSY APPROACHING THE ISLE OF WIGHT
"Zounds ! What risks we run to obtain such teas"

By Appointment to H.M. KING GEORGE V
H.R.H. The PRINCE *of* VVALES, *QUEEN*
ALEXANDRA & *The* KING *of* SPAIN

Tea flyer, 1929

A NEW ERA IN TEA

By this date Ceylon, now Sri Lanka, had joined
the ranks of tea producers, thanks largely to the
coffee crop failing in the 1860s. By the early 1870s,
India and Ceylon were jointly acknowledged as
the Empire tea growers. China never resumed her
preeminence after the Opium Wars, and Chinese
tea became the choice of specialist tea drinkers
which could only be bought in Fortnum & Mason
and other specialist grocers.

A ROYAL APPOINTMENT

Fortnum & Mason has long been linked with the
Royal Family. Generations of the Fortnum family
worked in Royal service, from the reign of Queen
Anne onwards. During the long and illustrious
reign of Queen Victoria the company received the
first of its many Royal Warrants. On 30 August
1867, the company was appointed Grocers and Tea
Dealers to her son, Prince Albert, HRH the Duke
of Edinburgh. Today the world-famous store
continues to hold a royal warrant for the Queen
for grocers and provisions merchants and as tea
merchants and grocers to the Prince of Wales for
the regular supply of a range of its products.

A few of Fortnum's teas have been created
uniquely for members of the Royal household.
The Royal Blend tea was developed for King
Edward VII and is a blend of Assam and low
grown Ceylon teas; the latter gives a lighter, more
uplifting note to the malty Assam. It is a strong
tea and is best drunk with milk.

The Queen Anne blend was created in 1907 on Fortnum's 200th anniversary to commemorate the reigning monarch at the time of the company's formation. The tea, with its bright liquor, is refreshing at any time of the day and is a blend of Assam and high grown Ceylon. Although Assam based it is slightly lighter than the Royal Blend and can be taken without milk.

A request from Buckingham Palace resulted in Fortnum's Smoky Earl Grey blend. This tea combines the traditional fragrant bergamot with Lapsang and Gunpowder and creates a unique brew.

The history of tea in Britain and the history of the house of Fortnum & Mason, tea dealers and grocers, are inextricably linked. Piccadilly was and is a destination for fine teas from far-away lands, and is the centre of excellence, knowledge and passion for the golden brew that defines a nation. Let us raise a cup to intertwining histories.

Opposite: The shop front, 2007
Below: The tea counter, 1990

Taking
Tea

Tea comes from the evergreen bush, *Camellia sinensis*, and is manufactured into black, green, oolong or white tea, depending on how it is processed. The terroir – climate, soil and topography – are key in winemaking and similar conditions are essential in tea growing, too. Just like wine, the quality of the leaves depends on when and where they were picked, the climate, the soil conditions and the altitude of the plants. For the tea plant to flourish it needs temperatures of between 10–27°C, and up to 2¼ metres of rainfall per year, combined with elevations of between 300–2000 metres above sea level, slightly acidic soil and good drainage. The main tea producers are countries that offer these ideal growing conditions, including China, which produces a mixture of green and black tea; India, which cultivates mainly black tea; Sri Lanka (formerly Ceylon), which produces mainly black tea; Japan for green and Taiwan (Formosa) for green and oolong, a semi-fermented or partially oxidised tea.

Fortnum & Mason offers a range of both large-leaf blended teas as well as a selection of the finest Single Estate Teas from around the world. A Single Estate Tea is a tea grown from one plantation only – not a mixture or blend of teas grown on several plantations. Many Single Estate Teas are classified as rare when they are either produced from only a very small number of bushes (some are over one hundred years old) or when only a very small amount of a particular quality is produced annually. (For more information on blends see pages 28–29.)

To produce black tea, once the leaf is picked it is taken to a factory where it is spread out on trays in very warm conditions (around 25–30°C) to wither. The withered leaf is then rolled to release the chemicals within the leaf that produce the flavour and colour of the drink, and set aside to absorb oxygen to complete the fermentation process. The leaf is ready for the next stage when it has turned a rich, golden, russet colour, when it is dried or fired to stop the natural decomposition process. It is at this point that the leaf turns black and is then sorted and graded (see page 25).

Oolong teas are semi-fermented leaves, and as such they are left to ferment for a much shorter time. There are many types of oolong, some are very lightly shaken to bruise the edges of the leaf and initiate a type of fermentation. The leaves are then rolled either into tight little knots or into long strands of tea. The delicate flavour comes from the soil, altitude and the care in processing.

Green teas follow the same harvesting and withering process, but once withered they do not undergo a fermentation process and are instead steamed or roasted to soften the leaves then rolled (many still by hand). This process is repeated and the leaves are left to dry.

White tea is the least processed of all teas. The leaves are picked before new buds open and they are spread out, usually to solar wither, before being dried. In the mid 1880s growers started to select specific varietals of tea bushes to make 'Silver Needles' and other white teas. The large, fleshy buds of the 'Big White', 'Small White' and 'Narcissus' tea bushes were selected to make white teas and these are (mostly) still used today as the raw material for the production of white tea.

CREATING THE PERFECT BLEND

Blending tea is just like bringing together the best grape varieties to make the perfect bottle of wine. Skill and knowledge are, of course, key to the job. Tea tasters train their palates so they can blend a variety of leaves to make the perfect brew. By doing this they are also maintaining a consistent quality.

Fortnum & Mason teas vary from being aromatic, such as Earl Grey and Lapsang Souchong; strong, like the rich and malty Assam and the invigorating Breakfast Blend; or light and delicate, such as Ceylon Orange Pekoe or Keemun.

TEA	CHARACTERISTICS
Keemun (China)	Produced in Quimen, Anhui Province. The most famous of the Chinese black teas; made from a congou – a well-twisted, thin, tight leaf.
Lapsang Souchong (China)	A smoked tea from the Fujian Province. Dried over smoking fires of pinewood. Large thin strips of black leaf.
Taiwan Oolong (Taiwan)	Large silver-brown leaves that produce a delicate, pronounced peach flavour.

TEA LEAF GRADING

Once tea has been picked and has arrived at the warehouse to store, it is graded by the tea blender. This grading does not indicate the quality of the tea, merely the size of the leaf, which is then used by the tea blenders to compile the finished tea. The grades, variables of Pekoe and Souchong, are known as leaf grades, broken grades, fannings and dust grades. When tea is graded as broken, it means the leaf is in smaller pieces, while fannings are the bits of tea left over after processing and are used in tea bags. The dust grade is the lowest grade and are the smallest particles of the leaf produced during the sorting process. Listed on page 30 is the range of grades.

It takes several years before a tea blender gains enough experience and expertise to blend Fortnum & Mason teas; he or she needs to have a detailed knowledge of each of the individual teas to put together the perfect blend. Each blend is made

INFUSION NOTES	DRINKING NOTES
Use 1 teaspoon of tea per person, adding the water just before it reaches the boil. Infuse for 5–6 minutes.	Rich brown liquor, lightly scented. Serve on its own, or with lightly spiced foods, rich sweet cakes or an evening snack.
Should ideally be made with water before it reaches the boil. Allow 1 teaspoon of tea per person and infuse for 5 minutes.	Drink without milk or sugar. Very refreshing in hot weather; also good with strong cheeses and rich stews of red meat and wine.
Allow 1 teaspoon of tea per person with water just off the boil. Infuse for 5–6 minutes.	Drink without milk or sugar. Very refreshing for afternoon or evening drinking. Good with desserts and light cakes.

according to a recipe and uses only the best ingredients – the finest individual tea leaves. The characteristics of a tea can vary depending on when it is picked – even on which day – and the blender must be able to identify this.

The aim of blending is to maintain a consistent quality throughout the year, taking into account any seasonal variations that may affect the profile of the many teas that Fortnum & Mason buys. Just as a recipe might need adjusting in terms of taste, the same is true of blending. Occasionally Fortnum's tea blenders will need to amend the formula to ensure the character remains the same. Small hand blends (miniature trials of what will happen in the factory) are made first and then, once the flavour profile is right, the tea blend is born. Before the tea is made available, though, the mini blend and factory blend are brewed again to check their quality matches.

TEA	CHARACTERISTICS
Lung Ching or Dragonwell (China)	Long, flat green leaves from West Lake, near Dragonwell Springs, in Zhejiang Province.
Gunpowder or Pearl (China)	Produced in and around Ping Shui, in Zhejiang Province. Rolled into balls which unfurl when infused.
Mudan or Peony, Green or Black (China)	Hand-bound teas from Anhui Province. Manufactured into green or black tea, then tied up into intricate flower-like shapes. This is very difficult and requires great patience and skill.. When infused the tea opens up slowly into pretty shapes. Sometimes a colourful flower also emerges from the centre of the bundle.
Sencha (Japan)	The leaves are hand-picked and are then steamed, rolled and dried until they become like green needles. The liquor is green with a subtle sweetness and fresh green scent.
Gyokuro or Precious Dew (Japan)	The pointed green needles from plants are shaded during growth to promote colouring. This is Japan's finest tea.

INFUSION NOTES	DRINKING NOTES
Use 2 teaspoons of tea per person with water at about 70°C. Infuse for 3 minutes.	A very fine green tea to drink throughout the day, or as a digestif. Drink without milk or sugar.
Use 2 teaspoons per person with water at about 75–80°C. Infuse for 3–4 minutes.	Refreshing tea for the afternoon and evenings. Drink alone, with mint or lemon. Good for sorbets and iced tea.
Use one 'flower' per person. Infuse in water at around 80°C for 5 minutes. Infuse and serve in a tumbler or a shallow white cup to show off its appearance.	Very refreshing. Drink as an afternoon tea or as a digestif, without milk or sugar.
Scant 1 teaspoon per person. Infuse in water at 70°C for 2 minutes.	Drink without milk or sugar, with or without food. Also a good digestif.
Use freshly boiled water which has cooled to 50°C. Infuse 1 teaspoon of tea in 4 tablespoons of water for 2½ minutes; add more water to taste or for further infusions.	Drink alone or after meals as a digestif. A very special tea – refreshing, slightly astringent and cleansing.

Special Finest Tippy Golden Flowery Orange Pekoe (SFTGFOP)	This is Flowery Orange Pekoe with the golden tips of the young buds; it is the very best whole leaf quality.
Finest Tippy Golden Flowery Orange Pekoe (FTGFOP)	This is Flowery Orange Pekoe with a high percentage of golden tips; it has an exceptionally high quality leaf.
Tippy Golden Flowery Orange Pekoe (TGFOP)	Flowery Orange Pekoe of exceptional quality.
Golden Flowery Orange Pekoe (GFOP)	The finest Flowery Orange Pekoe. This is the second grade of top-quality leaves with no tips, harvested once the buds have opened.
Orange Pekoe (OP)	This has long, pointed leaves that have been harvested when the end buds are opening into leaves.
Pekoe (P)	Shorter, less fine leaves than Orange Pekoe.
Flowery Pekoe (FP)	This has leaves that have been rolled lengthwise; shorter, coarser pieces than Orange Pekoe.
Pekoe Souchong (PS)	Shorter and coarser than Pekoe.
Souchong	Large rough pieces produced by rolling large leaves. This is often used for smoked China teas.

Broken leaf grades follow similar grading designated by a B; for example, Golden Flowery Broken Orange Pekoe is referred to as GFBOP.

Fanning and dusts are designated by F or D, thus Broken Orange Pekoe Fannings is referred to as BOPF, with BOPF1 being the top grade.

As well as looking at the flavour characteristics of the liquor, Fortnum & Mason tea blenders also look at the dry leaves for their style, shape and colour, as this also has to fit in within certain parameters. If the blender describes a leaf as 'common', it has no style; if it is 'bold', the pieces are too big to grade; if, however, it is labelled 'attractive' it has a bloom, is uniform in size, well made, and has a good colour with a sheen, and if it is 'coppery', this denotes a good-quality leaf that has been manufactured well.

To taste the tea, blenders use exactly the same method as wine tasters. First they take a mouthful of the liquor, then they draw in several breaths of air, slurping and swirling the mixture round in their mouths. This brings out all the individual nuances and flavours of the tea.

Terms for the tea liquor range from bright and golden (lively-flavoured brews with a desirable colour), to flavoury (denoting a distinctive taste). Malty is a characteristic found in good Assams, and pungent is used to describe a good Darjeeling, meaning it is astringent without being bitter. Some Assams can be likened to raspberry jam (yes, really!) and muscatel is a winning term for the finest Darjeelings.

HOW TO MAKE THE PERFECT BREW

To get the very best from your high-quality Fortnum & Mason tea, it is well worth following a few well-tested rules on brewing, as recommended by the experts.

First warm the teapot by rinsing it out with hot water. If you regularly drink a number of different teas it is worth investing in a number of different teapots as a patina will build up on the inside of the pot and will flavour the tea. It is generally considered that silver or terracotta deliver the best results for strong teas and bone china and porcelain work best for lighter teas. You should never wash your teapot in soapy water or through a dishwasher. After use the pot should be emptied, rinsed in detergent-free water and turned upside down to drain.

When it comes to how much tea to use, follow the rule of 'one teaspoon for each person and one for the pot' for loose leaves and experiment to find the ideal brew for you. If you are using tea bags, use the same guide: one bag per person and one for the pot. If you are brewing in a cup, use just one bag and leave it in for 4–5 minutes. Fruit infusions and green teas are normally drunk without milk, so 1–2 minutes is sufficient.

Use freshly drawn water when filling the kettle; if you live in an area with very hard water, filtering it first is advisable. The water should be boiling for black tea and off the boil (at 70–88°C) for green and white teas. If you're not going to enjoy all the tea in one pour, decant it into a second warmed pot, straining it as you do so. By separating the loose leaves from the liquor, this prevents the tea oversteeping and becoming bitter.

Traditionalists believe that putting the milk into the cup before the tea is best; this is because historically it protected the fine porcelain tea bowls when the hot tea was poured in and it also allows the two liquids to mix better. The scientific reason behind adding the milk first, though, is that it cools the tea and prevents the fats in the milk scalding and causing an unpleasant taste. If, however, you add the milk after pouring your tea, you can have better control over how much to add to achieve your preferred taste. All in all, we believe it's down to personal preference and probably makes very little difference to the actual flavour.

As a general guide, Fortnum & Mason's stronger teas (those blends made from Assam tea) are best served with milk. The lighter teas and aromatic teas are best served without, as adding milk changes the profile of the tea and will produce a different-flavoured brew. Although, again, it is entirely down to which way you prefer to enjoy your tea.

THE OLD SILVER TEAPOT

THIS is the tea we like to drink of a winter's evening when the curtains are drawn and there is no sound but the soft noises little flames make when they dance amongst the logs. We drink it slowly, savouring of its flavour and thinking of a thousand things. We peer curiously at ourselves acting the scenes of long ago, marvelling at the heat and anger that was once so real. Sometimes we unsay the things we would fain unsay and play again the part as we would wish it played—and then someone comes to clear away the tea.

Old Silver Teapot Tea, 3/6 per lb.

Being a blend of rare Indian,
Ceylon and Darjeeling Teas

10-lb. caddy 34/6, carriage paid

Inspecting General refusing Whisky-and-Soda and demanding Tea during the hot weather

Tea Commentary, 5th issue: Tea and Cakes, 1924

Royal Blend	Flowery Pekoe from Ceylon lends an uplifting note to make a traditional tea with a smooth, almost honey-like flavour.
Breakfast Blend	Unblended Assam leaves grown in the Brahmaputra Valley in Northeast India, make a strong brew with a malty, full-bodied flavour.
Regent's Blend	This bright, full-bodied blend honours centuries of dealings with China, India and Ceylon. A stalwart of the afternoon menu in our restaurants.
Afternoon Blend	A blend of teas from the higher and lower regions of Ceylon delivers a light, refreshing flavour with real body.
Piccadilly Blend	Recreate the experience of taking tea at Fortnum's with this refreshing Ceylon blend, usually taken without milk.
Earl Grey Classic	British Prime Minister Earl Grey gave his name to this popular tea back in the 1830s, and ever since it has been thought of as a classic English afternoon tea. It is not a type of tea, but a flavour, made up of a simple black tea flavoured with aromatic and stimulating oil of bergamot. Drink in the afternoon, and serve fresh without milk or lemon to ensure that you capture the top notes.
Countess Grey	Based on well-twisted orange pekoe teas, lifted by classic bergamot and a light orange flavour. Ideal for mid morning and early afternoon drinking.
Assam Superb	Assam Superb has a rich, dark liquor and smooth, round, malty flavour, and is ideal at any time of the day.
Darjeeling Broken Orange Pekoe	This justly famous black tea has a vivid, coppery infusion. The broken leaf grade gives a stronger brew that suits those who prefer to take their Darjeeling with milk.
Darjeeling Fine Tippy Golden Flowery Orange Pekoe	Made from leaf tips of the highest quality, it has a subtle Muscatel taste and a full-bodied and robust character, an ideal companion to a really special breakfast.
Russian Caravan	This light and nutty blend of China Black Keemun and Oolong teas recalls the trading routes that brought tea to the Tsars.
Fortmason	This blend of Indian and China teas is also perfumed with the delicate aroma of orange blossom to produce a subtle, floral flavour.

Rose, chamomile, lemongrass, raspberry, ginger and a range of dried herbs, fruit and flowers can also be used to make a refreshing hot or chilled drink – the correct term for these being an infusion or tisane. This is because they infuse the water with their essence, rather than needing to be brewed to release their flavour.

LOOSE LEAVES OR TEA BAGS?

The quality of loose tea is premium and loose leaves undoubtedly produce the best-flavoured brew. Tea bags are so readily available now that it's hard to believe they were introduced only just over a century ago, in 1908, in New York. The little silk pouches were originally made as tea samplers and were a quick and easy way of making a cup of tea. From silk came gauze bags and eventually paper. The bags also became a more compact size so they were easier to package and they were filled with fannings, or dust (a smaller grade of tea) to fill them, for a quicker brew.

The reason for the difference in quality is that the size of the bag restricts the size of the leaf and therefore tea bags lack the same complexity of flavour as loose-leaf tea. Despite this, the British public's appetite for tea bags was such that by the 1960s Fortnum's began to sell its own variety of quality tea bags. Today, approximately 97 per cent of the tea sold in the UK is in the form of tea bags, although, conversely, at Fortnum & Mason 70 per cent of the tea sold is loose leaf. To keep any type of tea at its best, whether it is loose or in bags, store it in an airtight container at room temperature.

We have Anna, seventh Duchess of Bedford (1788–1861), to thank for the ritual of afternoon tea, for it was she who created this delightful break in the day. At the time, she was one of Queen Victoria's ladies-in-waiting, and the royal household would breakfast well, lunch lightly and serve a great dinner late in the evening. The large gap between the midday morsels and night-time feast meant the duchess often experienced a 'sinking feeling' in the afternoon, so she asked one of her servants to bring her tea and cakes in her boudoir. She enjoyed it so much she called for it again and again. This custom is thought to have spread quickly through the grand houses surrounding St James's Palace, and also to Fortnum & Mason's Piccadilly store.

This new afternoon 'meal' fashioned a delightful collection of accoutrements that were required to serve the tea and its accompanying savoury and sweet treats. A teapot and a separate metal pot containing hot water were essential (the latter kept the water hot for refilling the teapot), and with them a jug of milk would be brought to the table along with a bowl of lemon slices. Individual strainers and holders were used for each pot and there would also be china cups and saucers and silver teaspoons to stir the milk and tea together. A china bowl for tea dregs was also on hand, so that each new cup could be enjoyed to the full. Sugar, despite not being everyone's preference, would have been offered as cubes in a bowl with sugar tongs to pick them up. Butter dishes containing pats of butter were served alongside a bowl of clotted cream and a bowl of jam, which were needed for scones. This elegant occasion also called for napkins, side plates and small dainty knives and forks with which to enjoy the morsels.

In the eighteenth century tea was an expensive luxury, so it would have been locked away in a tea caddy and the mistress of the house or housekeeper would keep the key safely secured on her belt. Caddies were produced in different shapes and sizes, but the most simple would have been a wooden box lined with

metal. Inside there were usually two chambers, each filled with a different tea. A glass bowl in the middle with a caddy spoon meant that the tea could be mixed to your own taste. More decorative caddies were also used to add to the sense of occasion of taking afternoon tea.

Caddies made wonderful wedding presents, with some of the most ornate being engraved with initials or impaled with coats of arms. By the Victorian era, tea had become much cheaper and so it was not so important to keep it locked away; however, the boxes continued to be used for many years to come as vessels in which to store and keep tea at its best.

Today, the art of tea combining has been revived, as discerning tea drinkers create their own favourite mixtures. The custom of taking afternoon tea – either by going out to do so or by enjoying it at home – has become popular again, with many different kinds of savouries, cakes and tea breads forming the basis of this delectable and indulgent occasion.

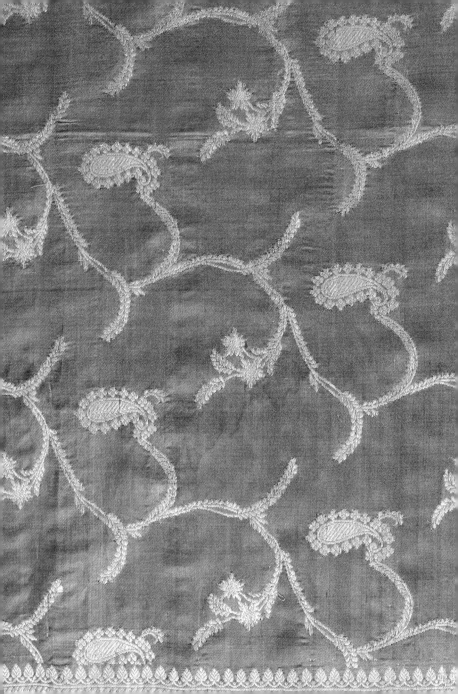

Sandwiches
and
Savouries

The Sandwich

Two pieces of bread holding a sumptuous filling
have developed over centuries into what we
have today. In its most simple form, in medieval
times, the essence of the open sandwich was born
when thick slabs of stale bread would be used
as trenchers or plates and the food piled on top.
It wasn't until the eighteenth century that the
sandwich got its name, from the fourth Earl of
Sandwich. He was playing a late-night game of
cards, so the story goes, and to prevent his hands
getting greasy he asked his valet to bring him
slices of meat tucked between two pieces of bread.

Cucumber,
CREAM CHEESE
AND DILL SANDWICHES

The seasoning for these sandwiches is key. Use a splash of white wine vinegar with the cucumber and add a little ground white pepper to the cream-cheese mixture; the acidity heightens the flavour of the cucumber while the pepper provides a savoury edge to the cheese.

**Makes 4 rounds
of sandwiches**

100g cream cheese

3 tbsp chopped fresh dill

A little freshly ground
white pepper

¼ cucumber, peeled
and finely sliced

1 tsp white wine vinegar

A little salted butter, softened

4 slices each brown and
white sliced bread

Mix together the cream cheese and dill in a small bowl and season with a little ground white pepper. Put the cucumber slices in another bowl with the vinegar.

Spread the cream cheese and dill mixture evenly over one side of the brown bread slices. Top with the cucumber slices.

Butter the remaining white bread and put a slice on top of each slice of brown bread.

Trim the crusts and cut each round into four fingers.

Smoked Salmon AND HERB CRÈME FRAÎCHE SANDWICHES

A light dressing of crème fraîche, soft herbs and mustard adds an elegant twist to these delicious sandwiches.

Makes 4 rounds of sandwiches

A little salted butter, softened

8 slices brown bread

125g thinly sliced smoked salmon

2 tbsp crème fraîche

1–2 tsp Dijon mustard

1 tbsp each fresh basil and parsley, finely chopped

A small wedge of lemon

Butter the bread then lay the smoked salmon over half the slices.

In a small bowl, mix together the crème fraîche, mustard and herbs, then spread over the remaining slices of buttered bread.

Squeeze a little lemon over the smoked salmon. Top with the other slices of bread and trim the crusts. Cut each round into three fingers or four triangles.

EGG AND CRESS *Sandwiches*

Creamy mayonnaise binding together egg and peppery cress is a delicious filling for nutty-flavoured seeded bread. These sandwiches are perfect with Fortnum's Piccadilly Tea, which is a refreshing blend made from Ceylon that is usually served without milk, or even as an iced tea (see page 124).

Makes 4 rounds of sandwiches

4 medium hard-boiled eggs, cooled

4 tbsp mayonnaise

4 tbsp cress

A little salted butter, softened

8 slices seeded bread

Salt and freshly ground white pepper

Tap the eggs all over to crack the shells, then peel. Put the eggs in a bowl and use a fork to crush them lightly.

Add the mayonnaise and half the cress. Season with salt and a little white pepper and stir to combine.

Lightly butter the bread, then divide the egg mayonnaise evenly over half the bread slices. Top with the remaining cress and slices of bread. Trim the crusts and cut each round into four fingers.

# *Chicken*
WITH TARRAGON BUTTER

The aromatic aniseed-like flavour of tarragon marries beautifully with a simple canvas such as roast chicken. These sandwiches are delicious as they are, or you can add another dimension to the flavour with a little of Fortnum's supreme Game Relish.

Makes 4 rounds of sandwiches

25g softened salted butter

2 tbsp fresh tarragon, finely chopped

8 slices walnut bread

4 tbsp Fortnum & Mason Game Relish (optional)

175g thinly sliced roast chicken

Mix together the butter and tarragon then spread it over the walnut bread.

Spread a thin layer of game relish over each slice, if using, and top with the sliced chicken.

Trim the crusts, then slice each round into three triangles and serve.

Afternoon Tea

A time-honoured tradition at Fortnum & Mason.
Served in the St James's restaurant, this wonderful
afternoon ritual starts with a savoury treat. Royal
Blend, Fortnum's most popular tea, is a robust
brew that makes a refreshing accompaniment
to all the savoury bites, combining low-grown
Flowery Pekoe from Ceylon and Assam. Earl
Grey is another popular choice – the citrus notes
of Bergamot complement any of the sandwiches,
particularly Chicken with Tarragon Butter. When
choosing teas to drink with your treats, follow
the culinary flavour rule and match like with like;
for example, the delicate taste of smoked salmon
works well with smoky Lapsang Souchong. If you
prefer a hot savoury, team the rich, lightly scented
and nutty flavours of Fortnum's Keemun Tea with
Welsh rarebit.

Welsh Rarebit

This classic teatime treat is seasoned with a dash of Worcestershire sauce, paprika for warmth and Fortnum's magnificent English mustard. Inspired by the classic pairing of cheese and nuts on a cheeseboard, we've served this on walnut bread, which makes a tasty base for the rich saucy topping.

Serves 2

25g salted butter

25g plain flour

150ml milk, warmed

75g mature Cheddar cheese, grated, plus a little extra

Splash of Worcestershire sauce

Pinch of paprika

1 tsp Fortnum & Mason Hot English Mustard

2–4 thick slices walnut bread

Heat the grill on a medium setting.

Melt the butter in a pan and add the flour. Stir together to make a paste and cook for 1–2 minutes. Slowly add the warm milk and stir together to blend. Bring to a simmer and cook gently until thickened.

Stir in the cheese, Worcestershire sauce, paprika and mustard, then remove from the heat.

Toast the bread lightly on both sides under the grill, then divide the sauce among the slices of bread. Top with a little extra grated cheese.

Put under a hot grill and cook until golden and bubbling.

Stilton
AND FIG TART WITH WALNUT DRESSING

These elegant tarts are a light but tasty alternative to sandwiches and would work well alongside a pot of Fortnum's Afternoon Blend Tea. Serve just warm or cold and dress with sprigs of watercress and a punchy dressing peppered with toasted walnuts.

275g all-butter shortcrust pastry

A little plain flour for dusting

25g salted butter

1 small onion, finely chopped

1 sprig of fresh thyme, plus extra to garnish

2 medium eggs

75ml double cream

Freshly grated nutmeg

2 fresh figs, each sliced into nine wedges

50g Cropwell Bishop Stilton cheese, crumbled

Salt and freshly ground black pepper

For the dressing

2 tbsp olive oil

3 tbsp walnut oil

1 tbsp red wine vinegar

25g walnuts, toasted and roughly chopped

A bunch of watercress

Preheat the oven to 200°C/400°F/gas mark 6. Roll out the pastry on a lightly floured board and use to line six 10cm round, loose-bottomed tart tins. Prick each base all over and chill for 15 minutes.

Melt the butter in a pan. Cook the onion with the thyme sprig over a low heat for 15–20 minutes.

Cover the pastry in each tin with greaseproof paper and baking beans and bake for 10–15 minutes. Remove the beans and paper and continue to cook for 5 minutes until the base feels dry to the touch. Reduce the oven temperature to 180°C/350°F/gas mark 4.

Discard the thyme sprig and spread the onion over the base of the tart. In a bowl, whisk together the eggs and cream and season well with salt, black pepper and nutmeg. Pour over the tarts.

Top each tart with three slices of fig and scatter over the Stilton. Bake for 20–25 minutes until golden and cooked through. Cool for at least 10 minutes.

Whisk together the oils, vinegar and walnuts and season. Put a tart on each plate, drizzle with the dressing and garnish with watercress and a few thyme sprigs.

Scones
and
Biscuits

Scones

These quick-to-make treats date from the 1500s and are originally from Scotland; oats were their main ingredient and they were round and flat and cooked on a griddle rather than in the oven. Scones became a feature of afternoon tea when, in the early nineteenth century, Anna the Duchess of Bedford chose them as part of the ensemble of sweet treats she requested for her afternoon snack (see page 36). In this recipe buttermilk provides the lovely flavour and light texture. You can leave out the sugar if you prefer a savoury scone and add a pinch of salt with the flour instead. These scones are best enjoyed on the day they are baked, warm, straight out of the oven and served with clotted cream and jam, but can be stored for up to a day in an airtight container.

Makes around 14 scones

85g chilled unsalted butter, cubed, plus extra to grease

250g self-raising flour, sifted, plus extra to dust

1 tsp baking powder

2 tbsp golden caster sugar

150ml buttermilk

1 medium egg

A little milk

Clotted cream and jam, to serve

Preheat the oven to 220°C/425°F/gas mark 7. Lightly butter a flat baking tray or cover it with baking parchment.

In a large bowl, rub the butter into the flour until the mixture resembles breadcrumbs. Stir in the baking powder and sugar.

In a separate bowl, beat together the buttermilk and egg, then make a well in the centre of the flour mixture and use a knife to stir all the ingredients together to make a soft dough.

Tip out the dough, lightly knead it on a floured board and roll it out to a 2.5cm thickness. Stamp out rounds using a 5cm cutter, transfer to the baking tray and brush the tops with milk.

Bake in the oven for about 15 minutes until well risen and golden. Cool until warm on a wire rack.

Serve with clotted cream and jam.

CHEDDAR SCONES

A spike of English mustard brings out the sweet punchy flavour of Montgomery Cheddar. Serve the scones warm from the oven, spread with a little butter and filled with cress and extra grated cheese. They are best enjoyed freshly baked, but can be stored for up to a day in an airtight container.

Makes 15 scones

40g chilled salted butter, cubed, plus extra to grease

275g self-raising flour, sifted, plus extra to dust

1 tsp baking powder

75g Montgomery Cheddar, grated, plus extra to serve

200ml buttermilk

1 medium egg

1 tsp Fortnum & Mason Hot English Mustard

Pinch of salt

A little milk

Butter and cress, to serve

Preheat the oven to 220°C/425°F/gas mark 7. Lightly butter a flat baking tray or cover it with baking parchment.

In a large bowl, rub the butter into the flour until the mixture resembles breadcrumbs. Stir in the baking powder and the cheese. In a separate bowl, beat together the buttermilk, egg and mustard with a pinch of salt, then make a well in the centre of the flour mixture and use a knife to stir all the ingredients together to make a soft dough.

Tip out the dough, lightly knead it on a floured board and roll it out to a 2.5cm thickness. Stamp out rounds using a 5cm cutter, transfer them to the baking tray and brush the tops with milk.

Bake in the oven for about 15 minutes until well risen and golden. Cool until warm on a wire rack.

Cranberry and Lemon SCONES

Sour cranberries and zingy lemon combine in these sweet fruity scones to make a match made in heaven. A sprinkling of cinnamon gives them a pleasing warmth. The scones are best enjoyed freshly baked, preferably straight out of the oven, split and served spread with a little butter, but they can be stored for up to a day in an airtight container.

Makes 14

85g chilled unsalted butter, cubed, plus extra to grease and serve

250g self-raising flour, sifted, plus extra to dust

1 tsp baking powder

2 tbsp golden caster sugar

50g dried cranberries, chopped

Zest of 1 lemon

½ tsp ground cinnamon

200ml buttermilk

1 medium egg

A little milk

Preheat the oven to 220°C/425°F/gas mark 7. Lightly butter a flat baking tray or cover it with baking parchment.

In a large bowl, rub the butter into the flour until the mixture resembles breadcrumbs. Stir in the baking powder, sugar, cranberries, lemon zest and cinnamon. In a separate bowl, beat together the buttermilk and egg, then make a well in the centre of the flour mixture and use a knife to stir the ingredients together to make a soft dough.

Tip out the dough, lightly knead it on a floured board and roll it out to a 2.5cm thickness. Stamp out rounds using a 5cm cutter, transfer them to the baking tray and brush the tops with milk.

Bake in the oven for about 15 minutes until well risen and golden. Cool until warm on a wire rack.

Jam BISCUITS

These bite-sized treats filled with sweet jam have a lovely crumbly texture due to the addition of ground almonds and hazelnuts.

Makes around 16

75g softened unsalted butter, plus extra to grease

60g golden caster sugar

1 medium egg yolk

15g ground almonds

15g ground hazelnuts

100g plain flour, sifted, plus extra for dipping

About 16 tsp Fortnum & Mason Rose Petal Jelly or Raspberry Jam

Preheat the oven to 170°C/325°F/gas mark 3. Lightly butter a baking tray or line it with baking parchment.

In a large bowl, beat together the butter, sugar and egg yolk with a wooden spoon. Stir in the nuts and flour to make a firm dough. Roll walnut-sized pieces of the mixture into rounds and put them on the baking tray.

Flatten each round and use the end of a wooden spoon dipped in flour to make a hollow in the middle of each one. Use a teaspoon to fill each with your chosen jelly or jam.

Bake the biscuits for around 30 minutes until just golden. Leave to cool on the baking tray then store in an airtight tin for up to three days.

Golden Crunch
BISCUITS

We have added a pinch of ginger to the recipe for these biscuits; the flavour is very subtle but it is just enough to take the edge off their sweetness.

Makes about 22 biscuits

110g unsalted butter, plus extra for greasing

125g plain flour, sifted

100g rolled oats

Pinch of ground ginger

¼ tsp baking powder

175g light brown soft sugar

1 tbsp golden syrup

Preheat the oven to 180°C/350°F/gas mark 4. Lightly butter two large baking trays.

Mix together the dry ingredients in a large bowl and make a well in the middle. Melt the butter, sugar and golden syrup in a pan with 1 tablespoon of cold water.

Pour the mixture into the middle of the dry ingredients and use a wooden spoon to mix well to form a dough. Roll tablespoons of the mixture into balls and flatten them slightly on the baking tray.

Bake in the oven for 12–15 minutes until golden. Leave to cool on the baking tray then store in an airtight tin for up to three days.

Rose Biscuits

These delicate biscuits, laced with rosewater and studded with crystallised rose petals, are as fragrant as a summer's day.

Makes around 20 biscuits

100g unsalted butter, softened, plus extra for greasing

50g golden caster sugar

1 tbsp rosewater

100g plain flour, sifted

50g ground almonds

15g crystallised rose petals, chopped

Preheat the oven to 180°C/350°F/gas mark 4. Lightly butter a baking tray.

Cream the butter, sugar and rosewater in a large bowl. Add the flour, ground almonds and rose petals and mix everything together to form a dough.

Take heaped teaspoons of the mixture and roll it into balls. Flatten them slightly on the baking tray.

Bake in the oven for 15–20 minutes until just golden. Leave to cool on the baking tray and store in an airtight tin for up to three days.

Macadamia
AND STEM GINGER COOKIES

The combination of the two sugars makes these delicious biscuits crisp on the outside with a slightly chewy middle. The macadamia nuts add a rich flavour and texture and the ginger brings an exotic bite.

Makes around 30 biscuits

100g unsalted butter

100g light muscovado sugar

85g golden caster sugar

1 medium egg

175g plain flour, sifted

½ tsp baking powder

1 tsp ground ginger

100g macadamia nuts

3 balls stem ginger in syrup, drained and chopped

1 tbsp stem ginger syrup

Preheat the oven to 180°C/350°F/gas mark 4. Line two baking trays with baking parchment.

In a large bowl, cream the butter, sugars and egg until soft and creamy. Add the flour, baking powder, ground ginger, nuts, chopped stem ginger and the syrup and mix all the ingredients together.

Drop heaped teaspoonfuls of half the mixture onto the baking trays and bake for 12–15 minutes until golden round the edges. Cool for a couple of minutes on the tray, then lift off with a palette knife and cool completely on a wire rack. Repeat with the remaining mixture. Once cool, store in an airtight tin for up to five days.

CLASSIC SHORTBREAD

Rice flour is the secret ingredient here – it gives the shortbread a wonderful crisp texture. Take care not to overwork the dough, otherwise the butter will become greasy and give an oily finish to the biscuit.

Makes 14 fingers

150g unsalted butter, softened, plus extra to grease

60g golden caster sugar, plus extra to sprinkle

150g plain flour, sifted

60g rice flour

Preheat the oven to 150°C/300°F/gas mark 2. Lightly butter a 17cm square tin.

Cream the butter and sugar together in a large bowl. Add the flour and rice flour and use a wooden spoon to work all the ingredients together to make a paste. Knead lightly.

Press the mixture into the tin, using the back of a spoon to smooth down the surface. Use a table knife to draw a line down the middle vertically, then mark six lines across horizontally to make 14 fingers. Prick each one with a fork.

Bake for about 30 minutes, then remove from the oven and mark again. Return to the oven and continue to bake for 30 minutes until the mixture is set.

Mark into 14 fingers again then sprinkle with a light dusting of sugar. Cool in the tin for about 30 minutes, then cut into pieces and carefully ease out of the tin. Finish cooling the shortbread on a wire rack then store in an airtight container for up to three days.

Florentines

These caramelised biscuits are rich, fruity and studded with nuts, while the rice flour gives them bite. After baking, one side is bathed in a layer of dark chocolate which complements the sweet toffee flavour perfectly. They are best enjoyed on the day they are made.

Makes around 22 biscuits

25g flaked almonds

25g hazelnuts, chopped

25g sultanas

1 piece orange citrus peel, around 25–30g, chopped

20g rice flour

40g plain flour

2 tbsp golden syrup

50g golden caster sugar

50g unsalted butter

200g dark Belgian chocolate, at least 50% cocoa solids

Preheat the oven to 180°C/350°F/gas mark 4. Line two baking trays with baking parchment.

Put the flaked almonds, hazelnuts, sultanas and citrus peel in a bowl. Add both the flours. Toss all the ingredients together.

Put the golden syrup, caster sugar and butter in a pan and place over a low heat to melt the butter and dissolve the sugar.

Pour the melted mixture onto the dry ingredients and stir everything together quickly.

Place half-teaspoonfuls of the mixture, well spaced, on the baking trays. Bake for around 12 minutes until golden around the edges. If any have spread together, use a knife to gently tease the edges apart. Cool on the trays, then use a palette knife to carefully lift them up and transfer to a wire rack.

Melt half the chocolate in a bowl resting over a pan of simmering water, making sure the base does not touch the water. Spoon a little chocolate over the Florentines and use a knife to spread it to the edges. Leave to set.

Melt the remaining chocolate, using the same method, then spread it over the first layer of chocolate. Leave to cool and when the chocolate has become tacky, use a fork to make a pattern on the base. Leave to set.

Mocha Shortbread
BISCUITS

The principle here is the same as for classic shortbread – you need to work all the ingredients together to make a dough paste. The combination of dark chocolate and one of Fortnum's finest ground coffees gives these little round biscuits a unique rich flavour.

Makes 16 biscuits

125g butter, plus extra to grease

40g golden icing sugar

25g dark chocolate, at least 70% cocoa solids, finely chopped

½ tbsp finely ground Fortnum & Mason Sandringham Blend Coffee

125g plain flour, sifted

40g rice flour

A little golden caster sugar, to sprinkle

Preheat the oven to 150°C/300°F/gas mark 2. Lightly butter a baking tray.

Cream the butter and icing sugar together in a bowl. Stir in the dark chocolate and coffee then fold in the plain and rice flours.

Roll walnut-sized pieces of the mixture into balls, place them on the baking tray, flatten them, then use the end of a wooden spoon to make a pattern around the edge of each. Chill for 5 minutes.

Bake in the oven for 30 minutes. Cool on a wire rack, sprinkle with a little caster sugar and store in an airtight tin for up to three days.

Small Cakes
and
Fancies

Madeleines

Proust immortalised these French scallop-shaped fancies in his work *Remembrance of Things Past*. Make sure you grease and flour the tin heavily so they come out cleanly from the mould, then enjoy them just as the French do – dipped in tea! Store in an airtight container and eat them within two days.

Serves 12

80g unsalted butter, melted and cooled, plus extra to grease

80g self-raising flour, sifted, plus extra to dust

80g golden caster sugar

2 medium eggs

½ tsp baking powder

Zest of 1 lime

Preheat the oven to 190°C/375°F/gas mark 5. Generously grease a 12-mould Madeleine tin and dust it with flour.

Whisk together the sugar and eggs in a bowl until thick and creamy. In a separate large bowl, combine the flour with the baking powder. Add half the butter to the sugar and eggs with half the flour mixture and fold in. Add the remaining butter and flour mixture with the lime zest and fold everything together carefully.

Divide the mixture among the moulds and bake for about 10 minutes until cooked and golden. Cool on a wire rack.

Tea Ceremonies

Tea is served all around the world, but in countries such as China and Japan it is a ceremony that is at the centre of their culture.

Cha Dao is the name given to the art of preparing tea in China, which involves preparing the brew in a clay teapot. The leaves are rinsed first in the pot with a little hot water. Depending on the type of tea, this is to remove any dust particles or to loosen the leaves to release the full flavour. Once rinsed, hot water – not boiling or it will affect the end result – is added to make the tea. It is traditional for the tea maker to pour the tea into small porcelain cups, filling them each halfway. Friendship and affection, the Chinese believe, fill the remaining part of the cup. Once each guest has a cup, it is customary to smell the tea, pour it into a drinking cup and sip it three times. The tea maker must ensure each cup of tea tastes the same.

The Japanese Tea ceremony, Chanoyu, is influenced by Buddhism. Chanoyu will often be held in a wooden or bamboo teahouse and there are a number of rules to follow, including being calm before entering the house, washing your hands, drinking from a certain side of the cup and placing it down in a particular way in front of you. It is a peaceful and reflective experience.

Blueberry and Vanilla FINANCIERS

There are two theories that surround the name of these delightful moist almond cakes. Some say it comes from the fact that they were popular in the financial area surrounding Paris's La Bourse du Commerce (Stock Exchange); others believe it is because they are baked in a rectangular mould which resembles a bar of gold. Store in an airtight container and enjoy within three days.

Makes 9

125g unsalted butter, melted and cooled, plus extra to grease

1 Madagascan vanilla pod

140g icing sugar, plus extra to serve

4 medium egg whites

50g plain flour, sifted

90g ground almonds

Zest of 1 lemon

A handful of blueberries

Preheat the oven to 190°C/375°F/gas mark 5. Grease and base-line the moulds of a nine-hole friand tray with baking parchment.

Slice the vanilla pod in half lengthways. Use a knife or teaspoon to scrape along the pod to extract the vanilla seeds. Add them to the icing sugar.

In a large bowl, whisk the egg whites until frothy. Add the icing sugar mixture, flour, ground almonds and lemon zest and fold everything together gently.

Spoon into the prepared tray and push three or four blueberries into each cake. Bake for 20 minutes until golden and a skewer inserted into the sponge comes out clean.

Leave in the tray for 5 minutes then cool on a wire rack. Dust with icing sugar before serving.

Éclairs
WITH FRESH CREAM AND RASPBERRIES

These little treats are made out of choux pastry, which is both quick and easy to make. Take care when adding the egg that you add only enough to make the dough smooth and shiny; if you add too much the finished éclair will have a heavy texture.

Makes 8

40g unsalted butter, chopped

100ml water

50g plain flour, sifted

1 large egg, beaten

For the icing and filling

50g unrefined icing sugar, plus 1 tbsp

150ml double cream

A handful of raspberries

Preheat the oven to 200°C/400°F/gas mark 6. Line a baking tray with parchment.

Put the butter and water in a small pan. Bring the water slowly to the boil, allowing the butter to melt. When the mixture is boiling fast, add the flour and quickly beat all the ingredients together. Remove from the heat and set aside to cool.

Add the egg, little by little, stirring until the mixture is smooth and shiny. Spoon into a piping bag fitted with a 1.5cm nozzle and pipe eight 6cm lengths of dough onto the baking parchment.

Bake in the oven for 30 minutes. Take the éclairs out of the oven, use a sharp knife to pierce a small hole in their sides and return to the oven for 5 minutes to cook on the inside. Cool on a wire rack.

Sift 125g icing sugar into a bowl and add a splash of boiling water – just enough to make a putty-like consistency. Slice each éclair through the middle horizontally and use a teaspoon to remove any uncooked mixture. Set aside the bases. Use a knife to spread the icing over each of the éclair lids.

Whip the cream in a bowl until thick. Add 1 tablespoon of icing sugar and stir in. Spoon the mixture over the bases of the éclairs and top with the raspberries. Replace the lids then arrange them on a plate and serve immediately.

Strawberries and Cream
CUPCAKES

A spoonful or two of double cream in both the sponge and the buttercream icing provides a sublime richness to the overall finish of these dainty cakes.

Makes 12

125g softened butter

125g golden caster sugar

2 medium eggs

125g self-raising flour, sifted

1 tsp baking powder

2 tbsp double cream

4 tbsp strawberry jam

For the decoration

75g butter

200g icing sugar, plus extra to dust

2 tbsp double cream

Fresh strawberries, to decorate

Preheat the oven to 180°C/350°F/gas mark 4. Line a 12-hole bun tin with standard-sized paper cases.

Cream the butter and sugar in a bowl until light and fluffy. Add the eggs gradually, adding a little flour if the mixture looks as if it is about to curdle.

Fold in the remaining flour, baking powder and double cream. Divide half the mixture among the cake cases. Put a teaspoon of jam in the middle of the mixture of each. Divide the remaining mixture among the cases.

Bake in the oven for 15–18 minutes until golden and firm. Cool on a wire rack.

Beat the butter and icing sugar together and whisk in the double cream to make a butter icing.

Spoon some of the icing on top of each cooled cupcake and smooth with a palette knife. Top with a strawberry and dust with icing sugar. Repeat with the remaining cupcakes.

Almond and Rose Petal SQUARES

These dainty almond bites are encased in shortcrust pastry and brought together with Fortnum's elegant Rose Petal Jelly. They make a delightful addition to afternoon tea. Store for up to a day in an airtight container.

Makes 16 squares

175g shortcrust pastry

Plain flour, for dusting

4 tbsp Fortnum & Mason Rose Petal Jelly

100g icing sugar

100g ground almonds

2 large egg whites

35g slivered almonds

Preheat the oven to 190°C/375°C/gas mark 5. Roll out the pastry on a lightly floured surface and use it to line a 17cm square baking tin. There's no need to grease the tin first.

Prick the pastry all over with a fork then spread it evenly with the jelly.

Mix the icing sugar and ground almonds together in a bowl. In another, large, clean, grease-free bowl, whisk the egg whites until stiff and then fold in the almond and sugar mixture.

Spread this over the prepared pastry and sprinkle with the slivered almonds. Bake for around 1 hour until golden brown and firm to the touch. Cool in the tin, then cut into squares to serve.

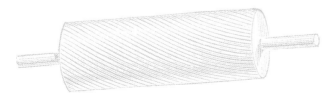

MACADAMIA AND WHITE CHOCOLATE *Brownies*

A soft squidgy middle is unique to brownies and is achieved by whisking the eggs and sugar until mousse-like, then baking only until the top is crisp. Take care not to overcook them or you will lose this unctuous texture and they will become cake-like.

Makes 25

200g dark chocolate, minimum 50% cocoa solids

175g unsalted butter

3 large eggs

225g light muscovado sugar

100g plain flour, sifted

100g macadamia nuts, toasted and chopped

100g white chocolate, chopped

Cocoa powder, to dust

Preheat the oven to 180°C/350°F/gas mark 4. Line a 20cm square cake tin with greaseproof paper.

Melt the chocolate and butter in a bowl resting over a pan of simmering water, making sure the base doesn't touch the water.

In a large bowl, beat together the eggs and sugar until thick and foamy – this will take around 8–10 minutes.

Add the melted chocolate mixture, flour, nuts and white chocolate and carefully fold everything together. Spoon into the prepared tin and bake for 25 minutes until the top is set and gives a little when pressed lightly. Cool in the tin.

Dust with cocoa, then cut into squares and serve. Any leftovers will keep well in an airtight container for up to five days.

Meringues
WITH DOUBLE CREAM AND LEMON CURD

Meringues are a unique confection, tasting of far more than the sum of their parts. Crisp with a slightly chewy texture, they are perfect sandwiched together with sweetened softly whipped cream rippled with lemon curd. Serve with a light tea, such as Fortnum & Mason's Keemun.

Serves 6

3 large egg whites

175g golden caster sugar, plus 1 tbsp to sweeten

300ml double cream

4 tbsp lemon curd (see page 121)

Preheat the oven to 130°C/275°F/gas mark ½. Line two baking trays with baking parchment.

Whisk the egg whites in a spotlessly clean grease-free bowl until stiff peaks form. Add the sugar gradually, continuing to whisk all the time until the mixture is glossy.

Use 2 dessertspoons to shape the mixture into ovals and place on the baking parchment to make 12 meringues. Bake in the oven for 1 hour until the meringues are golden and come away from the paper. Leave them in the oven to cool to allow them to continue cooking until they dry on the outside, leaving a delicious chewy centre.

Whip the double cream until thick then stir in 1 tablespoon of sugar. Add the lemon curd and fold in loosely to create a ripple effect through the cream. Spoon the cream mixture into a serving bowl and serve alongside the meringues for everyone to help themselves.

Plum and Almond
TARTLETS

A sweet short pastry provides a crisp base for the moreish frangipane filling in these irresistible tartlets. Push slices of ripe plum into the almond paste before baking, then finish with a glaze of Fortnum's signature jelly.

Makes 12
For the pastry
50g unsalted butter, chilled and cubed

100g plain flour, sifted, plus extra to dust

1 tbsp golden caster sugar

1 large egg yolk

❦

For the filling
50g softened butter

50g caster sugar

50g ground almonds

1 medium egg, beaten

2 plums, sliced

2 tbsp Fortnum & Mason Fortmason Jelly

Preheat the oven to 190°C/375°F/gas mark 5.

Make the pastry. Rub the butter into the flour until the mixture resembles breadcrumbs. Stir in the sugar and egg yolk with 2 tablespoons of cold water and knead lightly to make a dough. Chill for 10 minutes.

Roll out the pastry on a lightly floured board and use a 7cm cutter to stamp out 12 rounds. Use to line the holes of a 12-hole bun tray. There's no need to grease the tray.

Beat together the butter, sugar and almonds until mixed, then add enough egg to make a creamy mixture. Divide the mixture among the pastry cases. Push one slice of plum into each tartlet and bake for 20 minutes until the pastry is golden and the frangipane cooked.

Gently warm through the jelly then brush it all over the tartlets.

Caffeine in Tea

There is nothing quite as reviving as a good cup of tea. All tea contains caffeine, but in less than half the quantity of that contained in coffee. In addition, enjoying a cup of tea after a meal aids digestion as it stimulates the juices in the stomach.

If you prefer a lighter brew, the range of green and white teas at Fortnum's is unrivalled. Mellow and sweet, green tea is produced from the most tender leaves on the bush. These are steamed to prevent any fermentation and some believe that drinking it helps to promote good health and wellbeing. The delicate flavour of white tea is the least oxidized of all the teas, as it undergoes no fermentation and is simply briefly steamed. It is this production method, many believe, that enriches it with the health benefits associated with green tea.

For those who like to avoid any caffeine, there is Fortnum & Mason Royal Blend Decaffeinated Tea. This decaffeinated version is based on the famous blend created for King Edward VII in the summer of 1902. The tea, made from Assam and a dash of Ceylon, produces a smooth, almost honey-like flavoured brew and can be drunk at any time of day. Fortnum's uses the latest and best methods for decaffeination, with naturally occurring carbon dioxide removing the caffeine, without tainting the flavour of the finished product.

SOURED CREAM AND CHOCOLATE *Cupcakes*

Dark, rich and very moreish, these cakes are made with unsweetened cocoa powder, which gives them that essential depth of flavour. Pipe the icing if you fancy or spread it on with a palette knife and decorate with fine curls of white chocolate.

Makes 12

125g softened unsalted butter
125g golden caster sugar
2 medium eggs
100g self-raising flour, sifted
25g cocoa powder, sifted
A splash of milk

To decorate

25g softened butter
75g soured cream
150g icing sugar
40g cocoa powder, sifted
25g white chocolate, grated

Preheat the oven to 180°C/350°F/gas mark 4. Line a 12-hole bun tin with paper cases.

Cream the butter and sugar in a large bowl until light and fluffy. Add the eggs gradually, adding a little flour if the mixture looks as if it might curdle.

Fold in the remaining flour and cocoa with a splash of milk to make a dropping consistency. Divide the mixture among the cake cases.

Bake in the oven for 20 minutes until golden and firm. Cool on a wire rack.

Beat together the butter and soured cream, then add the icing sugar and cocoa gradually to make a thick icing.

Spoon some of the ganache on top of each cooled cupcake and smooth with a palette knife. Decorate with the white chocolate.

Classic Cakes
and
Gâteaux

Matching Teas and Cakes

At Fortnum & Mason we truly believe in pairing tea and cake in the same way that you would match wine with food. Just as it is customary to set off the robust character of red meat with a full-bodied earthy red wine, similar principles can be applied to our tea and cakes; the marriage of individual flavours allows them to complement and enhance each other.

If you like a strong tea, try Fortnum & Mason Royal Blend Tea and enjoy it with a slice of the classic Sacher Torte (see page 97). The full-bodied, smooth, malty flavour of the tea is the perfect match for the rich chocolate in the cake. However, if you are partial to a scone, team it with Fortnum's Assam Superb Tea. The plain flavour of this classic afternoon-tea treat (see page 54), whether spread with clotted cream and jam or butter, sits well with this rich, indigenous Indian tea.

Lighter teas are the perfect accompaniment to more delicate sweet treats. Fortnum's Keemun Tea, with its nutty liquor and scented undertones, is best enjoyed with Meringues with Lemon Curd (see page 81). If you prefer a white tea, such as Fortnum's prized White Yunnan Tea, pair it with Eclairs with Fresh Cream and Raspberries (see page 74) or Strawberries and Cream Cupcakes (see page 76).

Smoked, scented or spiced aromatic teas play best with spices. If your preference is for Fortnum & Mason Smoky Earl Grey Tea, combining bergamot with a little Lapsang and Gunpowder tea leaves, try the Honey, Sultana and Pecan Tea Bread on page 106. Rose Pouchong, with its floral fragrance is delicious with the Lavender and Honey Cake on page 113.

Madeira Cake

Madeira cake has a lovely firm sponge, which in this recipe is flavoured simply with lemon zest. A generous sprinkling with caster sugar before serving gives it a crunchy sweet crust. The cake got its name from the nineteenth-century tradition of serving it with a glass of Madeira or other sweet wine.

Serves 10

225g softened unsalted butter, plus extra to grease

200g golden caster sugar, plus extra to dust

1 tbsp vanilla extract

3 large eggs

75g plain flour, sifted

175g self-raising flour, sifted

Zest of 1 lemon

Preheat the oven to 170°C/325°F/gas mark 3. Grease and line a 900g loaf tin with greaseproof paper.

Beat together the butter, sugar and vanilla extract in a large bowl using an electric hand whisk. Gradually add the eggs, adding a spoonful of flour if the mixture looks like it is about to curdle.

Fold in the remaining plain flour, the self-raising flour and lemon zest using a large metal spoon. Spoon into the prepared tin, sprinkle with the extra sugar and bake for 1 hour until a skewer inserted into the centre comes out clean.

Cool on a wire rack and store, wrapped tightly in clingfilm, in an airtight container for up to three days.

Victoria Sponge

This classic cake, named after Queen Victoria, is usually filled simply with jam, but for a more indulgent confection spread whipped double cream or buttercream over the jam.

Serves 12

200g softened unsalted butter, plus extra to grease

200g golden caster sugar, plus extra to serve

4 medium eggs

200g self-raising flour, sifted

1 tsp baking powder

4 tbsp Fortnum & Mason Strawberry Preserve

A little icing sugar, to dust

Preheat the oven to 190°C/375°F/gas mark 5. Butter two 20cm round cake tins and line each base with greaseproof paper.

Beat together the sugar and butter in a large bowl until light and fluffy. Add the eggs gradually, adding a little flour if the mixture looks as if it is about to curdle.

Fold in the remaining flour and baking powder using a large metal spoon, then divide between the two tins. Bake for about 25 minutes until well risen, golden and just firm to the touch.

Remove from the tins and cool on a wire rack. Peel off the greaseproof paper, put one half on a plate and spread the top with strawberry jam. Put the other cake half on top, dust the top lightly with icing sugar and serve.

Coffee and Walnut
CAKE

This light sponge is laced with coffee and chopped walnuts and decorated with a sumptuous buttercream and a sprinkling of nuts. Serve with a full-bodied tea such as Fortnum's Assam Superb Tea; its smooth malty flavour is a perfect match for this rich cake. Store in an airtight container for up to three days in a cool place.

Serves 12

225g softened unsalted butter, plus extra to grease

225g golden caster sugar

4 large eggs

225g self-raising flour, sifted

1 tsp baking powder

50g walnuts, finely chopped

1 tbsp coffee essence

To decorate

100g softened unsalted butter

300g golden icing sugar, sifted

2–3 tsp coffee essence

2 tbsp milk

40g walnuts, chopped

Preheat the oven to 190°C/375°F/gas mark 5. Grease and base-line two 20cm cake tins with greaseproof paper.

Beat together the butter and sugar in a bowl until pale and fluffy. Gradually add the eggs, adding a spoonful of flour if the mixture looks as if it is about to curdle.

Fold in the remaining flour, the baking powder, walnuts and coffee essence, using a large metal spoon. Divide the mixture evenly between the prepared cake tins and bake for about 20 minutes until well risen, golden and just firm to the touch.

Remove from the tins and cool on a wire rack.

Whisk together the butter and half the icing sugar in a bowl until creamy. Add the remaining icing sugar, coffee essence and milk and continue to whisk until light and fluffy.

Remove the greaseproof paper from the cakes and put one half on a plate and spread over about half of the coffee buttercream. Put the other cake half on top and spread the remaining buttercream evenly over it. Sprinkle the nuts around the edge, then slice and serve.

Chocolate and Orange
MARBLE CAKE

This dense cake is flavoured with chocolate and orange and topped with a rich chocolate icing. When placing the two flavoured cake mixtures in the tin, make sure you run a skewer through both to create the unique marble effect.

Serves 10

200g softened unsalted butter, plus extra to grease

200g golden caster sugar

3 large eggs

200g self-raising flour, sifted

1 level tsp baking powder

Zest and juice of 1 large orange

45g cocoa powder, sifted

To decorate

100g dark chocolate, at least 50% cocoa solids, broken into pieces

35g butter, chopped

Preheat the oven to 190°C/375°F/gas mark 5. Grease and line a 900g loaf tin with greaseproof paper.

Use an electric hand whisk to beat together the butter and sugar in a large bowl until light and creamy.

Gradually add the eggs, adding a little flour if the mixture looks as if it is about to curdle. Fold in the remaining flour, baking powder, orange zest and juice using a large metal spoon.

Put half of the mixture in a separate bowl and fold in the cocoa. Drop a spoonful of each mixture alternately into the tin then run a skewer through both to create swirls.

Bake in the oven for 50–60 minutes until a skewer inserted into the centre comes out clean. Lift out of the tin and cool on a wire rack.

Once the cake is completely cool, decorate it. Melt the chocolate and butter together in a bowl resting over a pan of simmering water, making sure the base does not touch the water. Once melted, stir them gently together. Drizzle the mixture over the cake and leave to set for around an hour. Store in an airtight container for up to four days.

SUGAR-CRUSTED *Cherry Cake*

Succulent candied cherries and creamy pine nuts star in this heavenly loaf cake. Replacing some of the flour with ground almonds provides a light texture.

Serves 10

175g softened unsalted butter, plus extra to grease

200g Provençal glacé cherries, rinsed and cut into halves

50g pine nuts

Zest and juice of 1 lemon

100g ground almonds

175g golden caster sugar

3 large eggs, beaten

200g plain flour, sifted

½ tsp baking powder

50g crushed sugar cubes

Preheat the oven to 170°C/325°F/gas mark 3. Grease and line a 900g loaf tin with greaseproof paper. Put the cherries, pine nuts, lemon zest and ground almonds in a bowl.

Cream the butter and sugar in a large bowl until pale and fluffy, then gradually add the beaten eggs. Fold in the sieved flour and baking powder using a large metal spoon, then the cherries and nuts and finally add the lemon juice to give a stiff dropping consistency.

Spoon into the prepared tin and level the top. Sprinkle with the crushed sugar, then bake for about 1½ hours until a skewer inserted into the centre comes out clean. Remove the cake from the tin and cool on a wire rack.

Sacher Torte

The recipe for Fortnum's Sacher Torte dates from the 1950s, when the store was bought by Garfield Weston. Mr Weston did not like jam in cakes, so the Hotel Sacher in Vienna provided him with a recipe without jam; it has been jamless ever since. Here we are featuring the traditional version of the recipe.

Serves 12

150g softened butter, plus extra to grease

200g dark chocolate, minimum 50% cocoa solids, finely chopped

125g golden caster sugar

6 medium eggs, separated

125g plain flour, sifted

To decorate

200g dark chocolate

175ml double cream

2 tsp glycerine

3 tbsp apricot jam

Preheat the oven to 180°C/350°F/gas mark 4. Grease and line a 20cm cake tin with greaseproof paper. Melt the chocolate in a bowl resting over a pan of simmering water, making sure the base does not touch the water. Cool a little.

Beat together the butter and 100g of the sugar in a large bowl. In a separate bowl, whisk together the egg whites until stiff, then whisk in the remaining sugar. Stir the egg yolks into the butter and sugar mixture.

Add the chocolate and the flour to the mixture. Carefully fold everything together, making sure not much air is knocked out. Fold in the egg whites.

Spoon the mixture into the cake tin and bake for 45–50 minutes. To check the cake is cooked, insert a skewer into the centre – it should come out clean. Remove from the tin and cool on a wire rack.

Put the chocolate, double cream and glycerine in a bowl resting over a pan of simmering water, making sure the base doesn't touch the water. When the chocolate has melted, stir gently.

Remove the paper from the cake. Use a sharp knife to split the cake through the middle and spread the apricot jam over the base. Top with the other half of the cake then lift the cake onto a wire rack sitting on a tray. Pour the chocolate mixture all over the cake to cover, using a palette knife to guide it. Leave to set for around 2 hours. Store in an airtight container in a cool place. Enjoy within four days.

Hazelnut Roulade
WITH RASPBERRIES AND CREAM

This gateau uses just a drizzle of butter in the sponge, which creates a unique delicate texture. When rolling up, the cake will crack a little, but don't worry; it is meant to. Simply dust with icing sugar before serving and serve with extra raspberries scattered around the outside.

Serves 8

2 medium eggs

50g unrefined golden caster sugar

15g unsalted butter, melted and cooled

50g plain flour, sifted

75g hazelnuts, finely chopped

Icing sugar, to dust

To decorate

1 tbsp raspberry liqueur

150ml double cream

1 tbsp icing sugar

150g raspberries

Preheat the oven to 200°C/400°F/gas mark 6. Line a 30cm x 18cm Swiss roll tin with greaseproof paper.

Whisk the eggs and caster sugar in a freestanding mixer or with an electric whisk for 5 minutes until thick and foamy.

Fold in the butter with the flour and half the chopped hazelnuts. Pour into the prepared tin and bake for 12 minutes until risen and completely cooked.

Dust a clean tea towel with icing sugar and sprinkle over the remaining chopped hazelnuts. Turn out the cake onto the tea towel and leave to cool, leaving the greaseproof paper on the base.

When ready to serve, remove the paper from the cake and drizzle over the raspberry liqueur. Whip the cream until thick with the icing sugar. Spread the cream evenly over the roulade. Scatter over the raspberries. Roll up the roulade from the shortest edge and put on a serving plate. Slice and serve immediately.

Fruit Cakes
and
Tea Breads

ECCLES CAKES

Despite being called cakes, there is not a crumb of sponge in sight here. These crisp puff pastry treats hail from Eccles in Lancashire and encase a treasure chest of currants, candied peel, orange zest and spices.

Makes 6

50g currants

15g candied peel, finely chopped

10g unsalted butter, plus extra to grease

25g golden caster sugar, plus extra to sprinkle

A pinch each of nutmeg and mixed spice

Zest of ½ orange

375g ready-rolled puff pastry

Flour, to dust

Put the currants, candied peel, butter and sugar in a small pan and heat gently to melt the butter. Add the spices and orange zest and stir everything together. Cool a little.

Preheat the oven to 220°C/425°F/gas mark 7. Unroll the puff pastry on a lightly floured board. Use a 10cm plain cutter to stamp out six rounds.

Divide the currant mixture among the rounds, leaving about a 2.5cm border. Brush the edges with water and bring the pastry up and around the mixture, sealing the dough together and shaping it into a small round. Turn it over, with the seal underneath, and put on a baking tray lined with greaseproof paper. Use a knife to cut two holes in the top of the pastry, then brush with water, sprinkle with sugar and bake for 15–20 minutes until golden and crisp.

Tea Cakes

This enriched dough made with butter, milk, eggs and a little sugar gives these fruity buns a moreish soft texture. Resist adding any more flour when you are kneading the ingredients together; it should be soft and sticky. Bakers follow the rule 'the wetter the better'. Enjoy as they are or toasted and spread with butter, jam (see page 120) or a fruit curd (see page 122).

Makes 12 buns

15g fresh yeast or 7g dried yeast

250–300ml milk

25g golden caster sugar

550g strong bread flour

1 tsp ground mixed spice

75g softened salted butter

1 medium egg, beaten

100g mixed dried fruit, such as currants, sultanas and raisins

25g candied peel, chopped

For the glaze

1 medium egg, beaten

Granulated sugar

Put the yeast in a small bowl and add a splash of milk and a pinch of the sugar. Leave to activate for 5 minutes.

Put the flour into a large bowl or the bowl of a freestanding mixer. Add the mixed spice and remaining sugar and toss to mix. Warm the remaining milk until hand hot.

Make a well in the centre of the flour and add the frothy yeast mixture, the butter, egg and 250ml of the hot milk. Knead well to make a soft sticky dough – this will take about 10 minutes – adding in the extra 50ml milk if the dough needs it. If you are using a freestanding mixer, use the dough hook to do this – it will take about 5 minutes. Cover the bowl and leave in a warm place to allow the dough to rise and double in size.

Take the dough out of the bowl and stretch it into a rectangle. Tip the dried and candied fruit into the middle of the dough and wrap the edges over it, then knead well to incorporate all the fruit.

Preheat the oven to 200°C/400°F/gas mark 6. Divide the dough into 12 even-sized pieces and shape each one into a roll. Push any dried fruit that is exposed on top to underneath the dough, otherwise it will burn when the roll is baked. Put on a baking tray lined with baking parchment, cover with oiled clingfilm and leave in a warm place for around 1 hour to prove. It is ready when you press your finger into the dough and it springs back.

Remove the clingfilm and brush the rolls with beaten egg then sprinkle with a little granulated sugar and bake in the oven for 18–20 minutes until the rolls are golden and they sound hollow when tapped underneath.

Cool on a wire rack and store in an airtight container for up to three days.

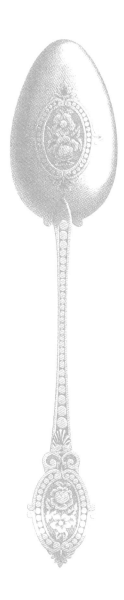

HONEY, SULTANA AND PECAN
Tea Bread

This is a moist and crumbly tea bread enriched with honey, mixed spice and the aromatic flavours of Earl Grey, one of Fortnum's finest teas. This cake will become firmer with time and stores well for up to five days in an airtight container.

Serves 10

200g sultanas

200ml freshly brewed Fortnum & Mason Earl Grey Classic Tea

75g softened butter, plus extra to grease

125g light brown soft sugar

2 tbsp set honey

2 medium eggs

200g self-raising flour, sifted

1 level tsp mixed spice

75g pecans, chopped

Put the sultanas in a bowl with the tea and leave to soak overnight.

Preheat the oven to 180°C/350°F/gas mark 4. Grease and line a 900g loaf tin with greaseproof paper.

Whisk together the butter, sugar and honey. Gradually add the eggs, then fold in the flour, mixed spice, pecans and soaked sultanas with any extra tea. Bake in the oven for 1 hour until a skewer inserted into the centre comes out clean.

Cool in the tin, then slice and serve.

Cooking with Tea

The partnership of tea and food dates back to ancient China, where tea was often used in savoury dishes. One such recipe involved adding the leaves to the fire when cooking duck, which infused a wonderful smoked seasoning in the meat. The Chinese would also stuff tea leaves inside fish, just as we do with lemon and herbs, before steaming, which similarly created a delicate aromatic flavour.

Tea goes hand in hand with baking – and not just as a brew alongside a cake. It works particularly well in fruit cakes, as soaking the dried fruit in freshly brewed tea produces plump pieces and gives the bake a pleasingly moist texture. You can also use a delicate tea such as Earl Grey to add a new dimension to biscuits, sponges and even ice cream.

Generally it is best to use a stronger brew in baking to allow all the aromatic notes of the blend to come through. When preparing tea to use in baking, pour cold or warm water over the leaves and set aside to infuse for 20 minutes – any longer and the flavour will become stewed and bitter and affect the taste of the baked goods.

DATE AND WALNUT *Loaf*

This loaf has a rich dark character with a zesty edge, due to the addition of the orange. Finish with a sprinkling of Demerara sugar and some chopped walnuts to decorate.

Serves 10

125g softened butter, plus extra to grease

100ml freshly brewed Fortnum & Mason Royal Blend Tea

50g dates, chopped

175g dark muscovado sugar

2 large eggs

75g wholemeal flour, sifted

125g self-raising flour, sifted

1 tsp baking powder

Zest of 1 orange

100g walnuts, chopped

1 tbsp Demerara sugar

Preheat the oven to 180°C/350°F/gas mark 4. Grease and line a 900g loaf tin with greaseproof paper. Pour the tea into a small bowl and add the dates. Set aside to soak while you prepare the other ingredients.

Cream the butter and muscovado sugar in a bowl. Gradually add the eggs, beating well after each addition.

Fold in the flours, baking powder, orange zest, dates and the tea and 75g of the walnuts. Spoon the mixture into the prepared tin and sprinkle with the remaining walnuts and Demerara sugar. Bake for 1 hour.

Cool in the tin for 10 minutes, then transfer to a wire rack to cool completely. This can be stored in an airtight container for up to five days.

Citrus Syrup
SPONGE LOAF CAKE

This simple sponge is enhanced with orange and lemon zest. It becomes beautifully moist when you pour over the orange and lemon syrup while the cake is still warm.

Serves 10

200g softened unsalted butter, plus extra to grease

200g golden caster sugar, plus 4 tbsp extra for the syrup

3 large eggs

100g plain flour, sifted

100g self-raising flour, sifted

Zest and juice of 1 orange and 1 lemon

Preheat the oven to 170°C/325°F/gas mark 3. Grease and line a 900g loaf tin with greaseproof paper.

Beat together the butter and 200g sugar in a large bowl using an electric hand whisk. Gradually add the eggs, adding a spoonful of flour if the mixture looks like it is about to curdle.

Fold in the remaining plain flour, all the self-raising flour, the orange and lemon zest and half the juice. Spoon into the prepared tin and bake for 1 hour until a skewer inserted into the centre comes out clean.

Remove the cake from the tin and cool on a wire rack. Put the remaining orange and lemon juice in a pan with the 4 tablespoons of sugar. Heat gently to dissolve the sugar. Drizzle over the cake and leave to soak in. Serve sliced or store in an airtight container for up to five days.

Tea Cultivation in Britain

Fortnum & Mason is the exclusive retailer of Tregothnan's Single Estate Tea, which is grown in Britain on the Tregothnan Estate, at the far southwest of the country in Cornwall. The conditions required to grow tea are mild temperatures, wet summers and acid soil. It was at Tregothnan 200 years ago that they first cultivated an ornamental variety of the tea genus *Camellia*. It is only in the last 10 years, after much research, that they have successfully grown tea to drink. The production is the same – the leaves are picked, withered and rolled to produce a fine, clean-tasting tea. It is only right that this esteemed estate, which has been in the same family since 1335, should join together with the historic store Fortnum & Mason.

Honey and Lavender
LOAF CAKE

Infusing the sugar with lavender sprigs and using Fortnum's delicious thick-set lavender honey gives this cake a lovely moist crumb and delicate flavour. It makes the perfect accompaniment to afternoon tea.

Serves 10

Lavender sprigs, to infuse and to decorate

2 tbsp Fortnum & Mason Earl Grey Tea

200g softened unsalted butter, plus extra to grease

175g golden caster sugar, plus extra to decorate

2 tbsp Fortnum & Mason French Lavender Honey

3 medium eggs

200g self-raising flour, sifted

1 tsp baking powder

Wrap two lavender sprigs and the tea leaves in muslin and bury the package in the sugar for at least a day or up to a week in an airtight container. Remove the muslin before using the sugar.

Preheat the oven to 170°C/325°F/gas mark 3. Grease and line a 900g loaf tin with greaseproof paper.

Whisk together the infused sugar, butter and honey until soft and fluffy. Add the eggs gradually, then fold in the flour and baking powder. Spoon the mixture into the tin and bake for 1 hour until a skewer inserted into the centre comes out clean.

Remove from the oven and sprinkle with caster sugar. Cool in the tin for 10 minutes, then cool completely on a wire rack.

Decorate with extra caster and lavender sprigs before serving. The cake will keep for up to five days in an airtight container.

Gingerbread
WITH PRUNES AND ALE

This firm cake has a pleasing spicy warmth due to the combination of two spices, ginger and cinnamon. The stout, the Fortnum's tea, the treacle and the dark muscovado sugar all deepen the flavour, while the prunes and nuggets of stem ginger provide a fruity presence. Store in an airtight container for up to five days.

Serves 12

100ml stout

100ml freshly brewed
Fortnum & Mason Assam
Superb Tea

75g dried Agen prunes

125g salted butter, plus extra
to grease

125g dark muscovado sugar

2 tbsp treacle

250g self-raising flour, sifted

1 tsp baking powder

1 tsp ground ginger

½ tsp ground cinnamon

2 large eggs, beaten

2 balls stem ginger,
finely chopped

To decorate

150g golden icing sugar

Put the stout, tea and prunes together in a pan and bring to the boil. Leave to soak for 1 hour. Chop the prunes roughly, reserving the stout.

Preheat the oven to 190°C/375°F/gas mark 5. Grease a 20cm square cake tin and line with greaseproof paper.

Put the butter, sugar and treacle in a pan and heat gently to melt the butter. Stir all the ingredients together then leave to cool a little.

Sift the flour, baking powder, ground ginger and cinnamon into a bowl. Add the cooled butter mixture with the eggs, stem ginger, chopped prunes and stout and gently fold everything together. Bake for 25–30 minutes until a skewer inserted into the centre comes out clean.

Cool in the tin for 5 minutes, then continue to cool on a wire rack. When the cake is completely cool, make the icing. Sift the icing sugar into a bowl and add a splash of boiling water to make it the consistency of double cream. Remove the greaseproof paper and spoon the icing over the cake, using a palette knife to cover the top. Cut into triangles and serve.

Apricot and Ginger CAKE

A truly sumptuous cake, based on Fortnum's very own Apollo's Muse cake, laden with dried fruit, apricots and stem ginger. A generous slug of Fortnum's finest cognac gives a lovely moist texture and makes a truly magnificent treat. Delicious eaten on its own or with a slice of crumbly Wensleydale cheese.

Serves 8

150g unsalted butter, plus extra to grease

75ml Fortnum's Grande Fine Champagne Cognac

125g dried apricots, halved

75g sultanas

75g Chilean flame raisins

75g currants

25g candied peel, chopped

5 balls stem ginger, quartered

125g Demerara sugar

A good squeeze of fresh lemon juice

100g plain flour, sifted

50g ground almonds

2 medium eggs, beaten

To decorate

3 tbsp apricot jam

About 11 dried apricots

1–2 balls stem ginger, sliced

Preheat the oven to 150°C/300°F/gas mark 2. Grease and line a 13cm, deep, round cake tin with greaseproof paper. Wrap a double thickness of brown paper round the edge with string.

Put the cognac in a pan and add all the dried fruit, the stem ginger, butter, sugar and lemon juice. Heat gently to melt the butter, then bring to the boil and simmer for 1–2 minutes. Cool for 10 minutes.

Mix the flour and ground almonds in a bowl. Make a well in the centre and add the cooled fruit mixture and beaten eggs. Stir everything together then spoon into the tin and level the surface.

Bake the cake for around 1 hour 45 minutes until a skewer inserted into the centre comes out clean. Cool in the tin for 10 minutes, then leave to cool completely on a wire rack.

To decorate, remove the paper and place the cake on a cake stand or plate. Heat the apricot jam in a small pan until smooth and melted. Brush about 1 tablespoon over the top of the cake and arrange the whole apricots around the edge, slightly overlapping, reserving one. Lay the stem ginger slices on the inner circle, slightly overlapping again, then finish by placing the remaining apricot in the middle. Brush the remaining jam all over the fruit. Store in an airtight container for up to two weeks.

Preserves
and
Drinks

Strawberry Jam

The perfect conserve for freshly baked scones (see page 54). Strawberries are low in pectin, the natural gelling agent which helps jam to set, so you need to use a special jam sugar with added pectin to ensure it thickens and the strawberries distribute evenly throughout. Warming the sugar first ensures it dissolves easily and more quickly when you add it to the pan.

Makes 1.2kg (6 x 200g jars)

500g small strawberries

550g jam sugar with pectin, warmed

Zest and juice of ½ lemon

The seeds from 1 vanilla pod

A knob of butter

Wash and hull the strawberries. Put them in a preserving pan with the sugar, lemon zest and juice and the vanilla seeds. Place the pan over a low heat to gently dissolve the sugar, and stir with a wooden spoon to help it on its way. Pop a couple of saucers in the freezer.

Increase the heat and bring the mixture to a rolling boil. Boil gently for 3–4 minutes until setting point is reached. To test for a set, take the pan off the heat and spoon some of the jam onto a cold saucer. Draw your finger across the middle – if it wrinkles, it's ready to pot.

Stir in the butter and skim off any scum that's still lying on the surface. Allow to stand for 10 minutes then spoon into hot sterilised jars, top with waxed discs and seal with lids. The jam will store for up to a year in a cool place.

Lemon Curd

A zingy, creamy preserve, perfect for hot buttered tea cakes (see page 104) and delicious with warm Cranberry and Lemon Scones (see page 58). The curd can be kept for up to two weeks in the fridge.

Makes around 550g

Zest and juice of 2 lemons
(around 150ml)

3 medium eggs

175g golden caster sugar

100g unsalted butter, cubed
and chilled

Put the lemon zest and juice in a large bowl with the eggs and sugar. Stir everything together with a wooden spoon. Add the butter then place the bowl over a large pan of simmering water, making sure the base does not touch the water.

Stir gently, allowing the butter to melt and the mixture to thicken, for about 15 minutes. The curd is ready when the mixture coats the back of the spoon. Strain, then pot into hot sterilised jars, top with waxed discs and seal with lids. Cool, then refrigerate and enjoy within two weeks.

Lime AND PASSION FRUIT CURD

This exotic-flavoured curd is perfect spread between the layers of a Victoria sponge as an alternative to jam, or folded into whipped double cream to marry together two meringue halves. There is a perfect balance between the passion fruit and lime in this, so it is sweet and tart in equal proportions.

Makes around 550g

6 passion fruit

Zest and juice of 2 juicy limes

3 medium eggs

175g golden caster sugar

100g unsalted butter, chopped

Cut the passion fruit in half and scoop the seeds and juice into a sieve resting over a large heatproof bowl. Stir to extract the juice, then discard the seeds.

Add the lime zest and juice to the passion fruit juice with the eggs and sugar. Stir everything together. Add the butter, then place the bowl over a large pan of simmering water, making sure the base doesn't touch the water.

Stir gently and cook, allowing the butter to melt and the mixture to thicken, for about 15 minutes. The curd is ready when the mixture coats the back of the spoon. Strain, then pot into boiling hot sterilised jars, top with waxed discs and seal with lids. Cool, then refrigerate. The curd can be kept for up to two weeks in the fridge.

Iced Tea

Drinking iced tea is a delicious way to cool down on a warm summer's day and Fortnum's Piccadilly Blend is the perfect tea to use. Made from Ceylon tea, it produces a wonderful clear brew and a refreshing taste. Prepare iced tea in the same way as hot tea, by leaving the tea to infuse until the desired strength, then strain it and allow the mixture to cool completely. Add plenty of ice to chill and flavourings such as mint, lemongrass or Angostura bitters to taste. If you're using one of Fortnum's fruit teas, add a sprinkling of sugar to enhance the flavour of the fruit.

SEVILLE ORANGE AND WHISKY
Marmalade

Homemade Seville marmalade is a treat and makes the best use of bitter
Seville oranges, which are in season for just a few weeks at the start of each
year. This recipe calls for two different types of sugar, which provides richness,
while a glug of whisky gives a delightful depth of flavour.

Makes 2.4kg

1kg Seville oranges

1.5kg golden granulated
sugar

500g light muscovado sugar

75ml whisky

Wash the oranges, then cut them in half and
squeeze out the juice. If you use an electric juicer,
it halves the time it takes and removes all the pith
and pips, too – set these aside in a bowl. If you are
squeezing by hand, after extracting the juice, use
a spoon to scoop out all of the pith and pips. Put
them in a square of muslin and secure with string.

Finely slice the orange rind and put it in a
preserving pan with the juice. Tie the string of the
muslin bag to the handle and let the bag sit on the
bottom of the pan. Add 2.3 litres of cold water.
Bring to the boil slowly and simmer gently until
the rind is soft and the liquid has reduced by about
a half. This will take between 1 and 2 hours.

Add the sugar and heat gently to dissolve, stirring
to help it on its way. Put a couple of saucers in the
freezer to chill quickly.

Increase the heat and boil gently for 15 minutes
until setting point is reached. To test for a set,
take the pan off the heat and put a spoonful of the
marmalade on the chilled saucer. Draw your finger
across the marmalade. If it wrinkles, stir in the
whisky. Continue to boil for 5 minutes until setting
point is reached again.

Spoon into hot sterilised jars, top with a waxed
disc, then seal with a lid. The marmalade will keep,
sealed, for up to a year in a cool place.

Fresh Lemonade

Zingy lemonade is the perfect refresher on a warm summer's day. This recipe makes a slightly sweet drink, so if you prefer a sharper taste, add the juice of another lemon.

Makes around 450ml cordial

200g unrefined golden caster sugar

Zest and juice of 4 ripe lemons

Sparkling water, to serve

Put the sugar in a pan with 250ml cold water. Heat gently to dissolve the sugar. Bring to the boil and simmer for 2–3 minutes to make a lovely golden syrup.

Add the lemon zest and juice and stir everything together. Leave to cool.

Pour 25ml cordial into a glass, add ice, then top up with sparkling water. The cordial will keep in the fridge for up to five days.

Index